OFF-GRID GETAWAYS
Organic Architecture

© 2022 Monsa Publications

First edition in 2022 April by Monsa Publications,
Gravina 43 (08930) Sant Adrià de Besós.
Barcelona (Spain)
T +34 93 381 00 93
www.monsa.com monsa@monsa.com

Project director Anna Minguet.
Art director & Layout Eva Minguet.
(Monsa Publications)

Printed in Spain by Cachiman Gráfic.
Translation by SomosTraductores.

Shop online:
www.monsashop.com

Follow us!
Instagram @monsapublications

ISBN 978-84-17557-51-5
D.L. B 6196-2022

OFF-GRID GETAWAYS
Organic Architecture

monsa

INTRODUCTION

The multiple signals coming from all corners of the planet, represents a new warning for the awareness of the need to promote global policies that protect the environment in all areas. In this sense, the responsibility of architecture with society acquires a special protagonism.

The projects presented in this book, coming from nineteen countries on four continents, illustrate the multiple possible approaches that architecture uses around the world in search of sustainable and environmental preservation strategies and their application in the design and construction of single-family homes. With the support of the most modern technology or using traditional resources and techniques, the small scale of the domestic environment becomes a fantastic test to develop tools aimed at promoting energy efficiency, recycling and reuse of materials, social sustainability, respect for nature and the harmonious integration of architecture in a natural environment increasingly punished.

Las múltiples señales que llegan desde todos los rincones del planeta, representa un nuevo aviso para la toma de conciencia hacia la necesidad de promover políticas a nivel global que protejan el medio ambiente en todos los ámbitos. En este sentido, la responsabilidad de la arquitectura con la sociedad adquiere un especial protagonismo.

Los proyectos presentados en este libro, procedentes de diferentes países de cuatro continentes, ilustran las múltiples aproximaciones posibles que alrededor del mundo utiliza la arquitectura en búsqueda de estrategias sostenibles y de preservación del medio ambiente y su aplicación en el diseño y construcción de viviendas unifamiliares. Con el apoyo de la más moderna tecnología o utilizando recursos y técnicas tradicionales, la pequeña escala del ámbito doméstico se convierte en un fantástico banco de pruebas para desarrollar herramientas destinadas a fomentar la eficiencia energética, el reciclaje y reutilización de materiales, la sostenibilidad social, el respeto por la naturaleza y la integración armoniosa de la arquitectura en un entorno natural cada vez más castigado.

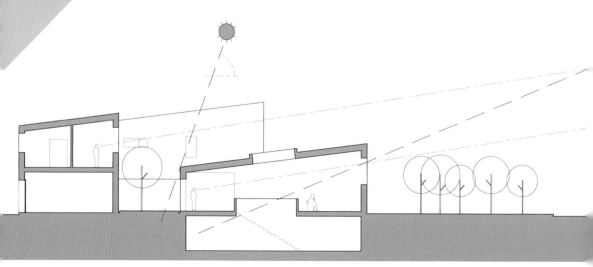

INDEX

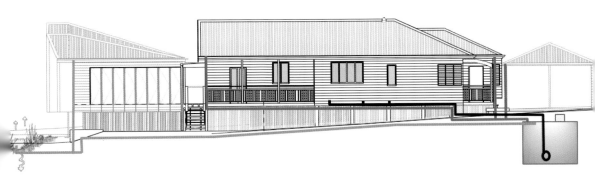

BRIDGE HOUSE
BIO ARCHITECTS

www.bio-architects.com
Architects: Ivan Ovchinnikov
Location: Tula Region, Russia
Total built area: 117 m2
Photo credits: © Artem Lasovskiy, Ivan Ovchinnikov

Out of comfort zone.
You always need to go beyond your limits in order to be succussfull in business, art or any other field. We are going in the mountains, swimming in the oceans, falling in love, discovering new places in order to feel something new.
This project has become a challenge for us and an unexpectable decision for a client. The idea of the second house on site was transformed into a game of the wooden structure between two banches.
The internal space that was formed by the structure has become the wide open place for creative work. All the loadcarrying structure is made of wood. There is a living room with the kitchen, two sleeping rooms with the bathrooms and sleeping spaces on the second floor of the living room.
"People are lonely because they build walls instead of bridges" (Joseph Fort Newton).

Fuera de la zona de confort.
Siempre tienes que ir más allá de tus límites para tener éxito en los negocios, el arte o cualquier otro campo. Vamos a las montañas, nadamos en los océanos, nos enamoramos, descubrimos nuevos lugares para sentir algo nuevo.
Este proyecto se ha convertido en un reto para nosotros y en una decisión inexplicable para un cliente. La idea inicial de una segunda casa se transformó en un juego de la estructura de madera entre dos bancos.
El espacio interior formado por la estructura se ha convertido en el espacio abierto para el trabajo creativo. Toda la estructura portante es de madera. Hay una sala de estar con la cocina, dos dormitorios con los baños y espacios para dormir en el segundo piso de la sala de estar.
«La gente se siente sola porque construye muros en lugar de puentes» (Joseph Fort Newton).

Conceptual rendering

Elevation

12

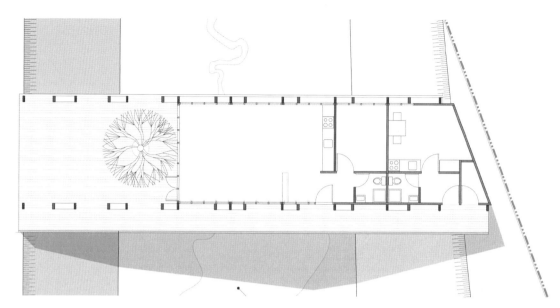

Ground floor plan

IREKUA ANATANI
BROISSIN M. ARCH. GERARDO BROISSIN

www.broissin.com
Project team: Arq. Adrian Tellez (project leader), M. Arch. Gerardo Broissin,
Arq. Mauricio Cristóbal, Arq. Alejandro Rocha, Arq. Adrian Tellez,
Arq. Thelma Blake, Arq. Luis Alberto Barrera
Location: Avándaro, Estado de México
Total built area: 700 m2
Photo credits: © Alexandre d' La Roche
General contractor: Miguel Campero
Suppliers: Furniture: Marina Pani
Consultants: Structural
Engineering: Ing Humberto Girón

Situated in a spot of colourful trees and sloping topography, the house adapts its shape and programme to the site to enjoy and preserve it. Its name, "family house under the trees" in the language of the Tarascan Indians, describes the starting concept of the project.

The building is oriented to adapt to the temperate and semi-humid climate of the area. The linear and opaque south-east façade is characterised by a curtain of wooden slats that sifts solar radiation. In contrast, the southwest façade, mainly made of glass, captures the afternoon sun. The open layout of the north façade, oriented towards a lake, reinforces the intention to live holistically with the environment. The fifth façade is 100% green, which maintains a uniform temperature in the ceilings throughout the year and camouflages the residence in its context, the original goal of the design.

Situada en un paraje de vistosos árboles y topografía en pendiente, la casa adapta su forma y programa al emplazamiento para disfrutar de él y preservarlo. Su nombre, «casa familiar bajo los árboles» en lengua de los indígenas tarascos, describe el concepto de partida del proyecto.

El edificio se orienta para adecuarse al clima templado y semihúmedo de la zona. La fachada sureste, lineal y opaca, se caracteriza por una cortina de lamas de madera que tamiza la radiación solar. En contraste, la fachada suroeste, principalmente de vidrio, captura el sol de la tarde. La disposición abierta de la fachada norte, orientada hacia un lago, refuerza la intención de vivir de manera holística con el entorno. La quinta fachada es 100% verde, lo que mantiene una temperatura uniforme en los techos durante todo el año y camufla la residencia en su contexto, objetivo original del diseño.

Front elevation

Cross section

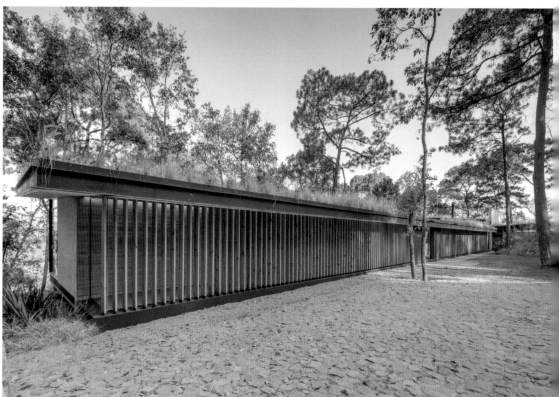

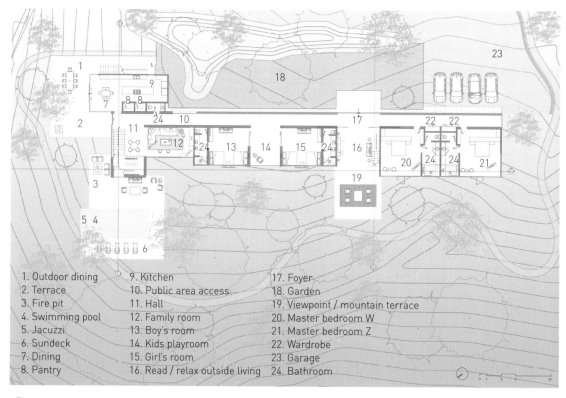

1. Outdoor dining
2. Terrace
3. Fire pit
4. Swimming pool
5. Jacuzzi
6. Sundeck
7. Dining
8. Pantry
9. Kitchen
10. Public area access
11. Hall
12. Family room
13. Boy's room
14. Kids playroom
15. Girl's room
16. Read / relax outside living
17. Foyer
18. Garden
19. Viewpoint / mountain terrace
20. Master bedroom W
21. Master bedroom Z
22. Wardrobe
23. Garage
24. Bathroom

Floor plan

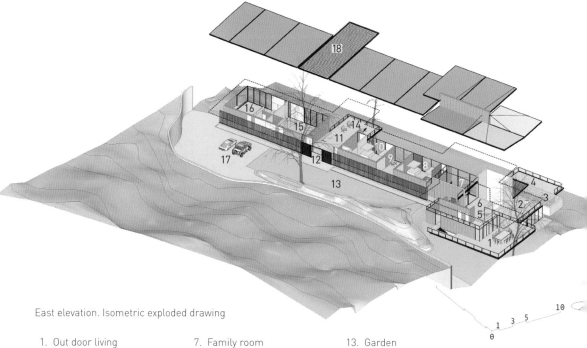

East elevation. Isometric exploded drawing

1. Out door living
2. Fire pit
3. Swimming pool
4. Sundeck
5. Kitchen
6. Hall
7. Family room
8. Boy's room
9. Kids playroom
10. Girl's room
11. Read / relax outside living
12. Foyer
13. Garden
14. Viewpoint / mountain terrace
15. Master bedroom W
16. Master bedroom Z
17. Garage
18. Green roof

West elevation. Isometric exploded drawing

1. Out door living
2. Fire pit
3. Swimming pool
4. Sundeck
5. Kitchen
6. Hall
7. Family room
8. Boy's room
9. Kids playroom
10. Girl's room
11. Read / relax outside living
12. Foyer
13. Garden
14. Viewpoint
15. Master bedroom W
16. Master bedroom Z
17. Gym and steam room
18. Guest rooms
19. Garage
20. Green roof

CASAS MQ
ALTAMAREA ARQUITECTURA

www.alta-marea.cl
Project team: Gonzalo Herreros Montero
Location: Punta de lobos, Pichilemu
Total built area: 290 m2
Photo credits: © Felipe Cantillana

The project comprises two houses of equal height and similar architectural style, which are located on the plot so that the views are not interrupted. The main house rests on the highest hill of the plot, while the second is raised on a concrete plinth for parking, which allows to equalize the levels of the floors of both houses. The floor structure is developed in modules of 3 to 4m in order to optimize the materials, mainly wood.

The images of both houses are joined through materials and textures, consid- ering similar details in both constructions. Structures and exposed beams are privileged together with materials such as wood, metal and exposed concrete. The finishes are worked in a rough way, seeking not to hide the nobility of the materials, leaving their elements to be shown as such.

El proyecto comprende dos casas de igual altura y de similar estilo arquitectónico, que se sitúan en la parcela de forma que no se interrumpan las vistas. La casa principal se posa sobre la loma más alta del solar, mientras que la segunda se alza sobre un zócalo de hormigón destinado a estacionamiento, hecho que permite igualar los niveles de las plantas de ambas casas. La estructura de piso se desarrolla en módulos de 3 a 4 m para de optimizar los materiales, principalmente madera.

Las imágenes de ambas casas se unen a través de materiales y texturas, considerando detalles similares en ambas construcciones. Se privilegia las estructuras y envigados a la vista conjuntamente con materiales como la madera, el metal y hormigón visto. Los acabados se trabajan de forma tosca, buscando no esconder la nobleza de los materiales, dejando que sus elementos se muestren como tal.

Site plan

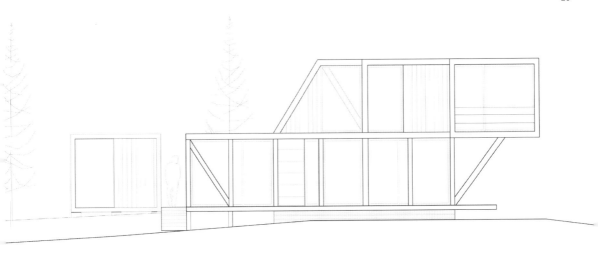

West elevation MQ house

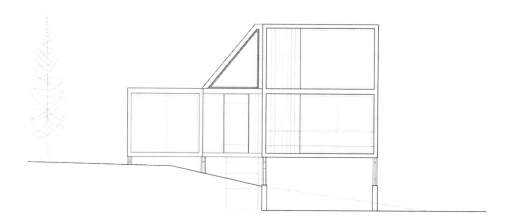

West elevation MQ2 house

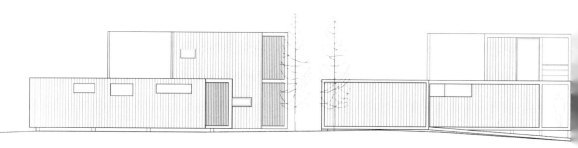

North elevation MQ houses

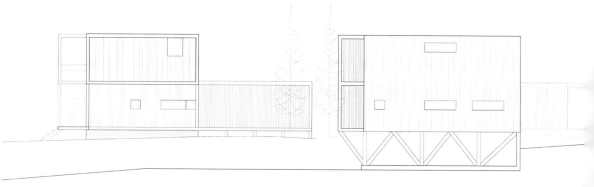

South elevation MQ houses

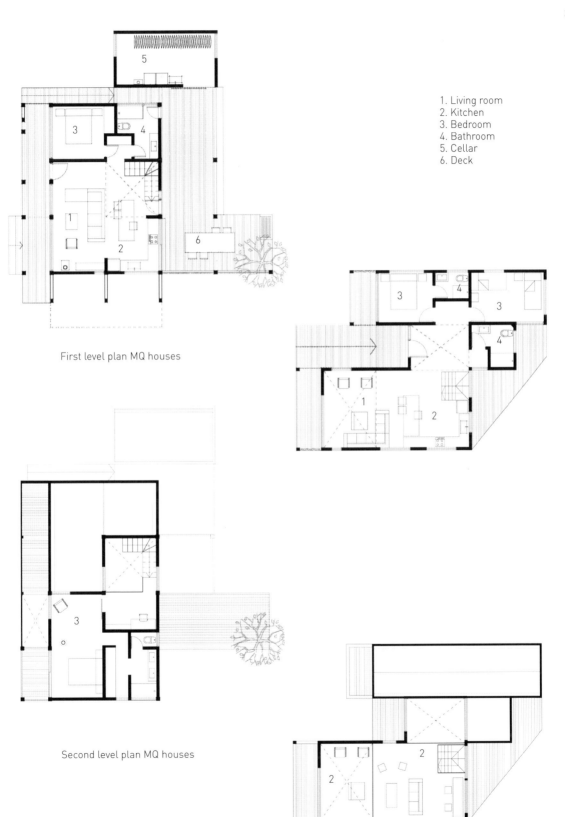

1. Living room
2. Kitchen
3. Bedroom
4. Bathroom
5. Cellar
6. Deck

First level plan MQ houses

Second level plan MQ houses

VILLA RAKU
DELIN ARKITEKTKONTOR

www.delinarkitektkontor.se
Project team: Buster Delin
Location: Risvägen 54, Nacka, Sweden
Total built area: 240 m2
Photo credits: © Karin Björkquist

Located on top of a lush hill, this two-story home also houses workspaces for its two owners, a potter and a garden designer. An important factor in the de- sign of the house was the use of the heat generated by the pottery ovens located on the lower floor, which accumulates in the intermediate concrete slab and is released on the upper floor, providing a comfortable and uniform temperature. The house was built on a grid of wooden pillars 2.35 m apart, which gives character and a clear rhythm to the design, forming a system in which interior and exterior walls as well as windows and doors are inserted.
Villa Raku is a house that is well integrated into its surroundings. It minimises its ecological footprint and in which two people can live and work with a creative lifestyle.

Ubicada en lo alto de una frondosa colina, esta vivienda de dos plantas alberga también espacios de trabajo para sus dos propietarios, un alfarero y un diseñador de jardines. Un factor importante del diseño de la casa fue el aprovechamiento del calor generado por los hornos de alfarería situados en la planta inferior, que se acumula en el forjado intermedio de hormigón y es liberado en el piso superior, proporcionando una temperatura confortable y uniforme. La casa se construyó sobre una retícula de pilares de madera de 2,35 m de separación, que da carácter y un ritmo claro al diseño, y que forma un sistema en el que se insertan muros interiores y exteriores así como ventanas y puertas.
Villa Raku es una casa bien integrada en su entorno, que minimiza su huella ecológica y en la que dos personas pueden vivir y trabajar con un estilo de vida centrado en la creatividad.

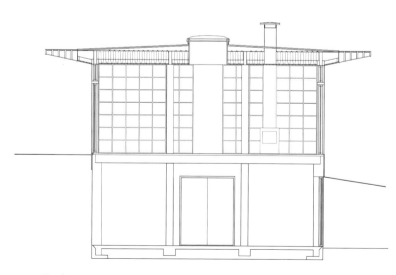

Sections

Sections

1. Main entrance
2. Studio
3. WC
4. Storing
5. Kitchen
6. Pantry
7. Dining / living area
8. Book shelves
9. Bedroom
10. Bathroom
11. Pottery
12. Oven room
13. Glazing room
14. Technical
15. Office
16. Guest room
17. Bathroom

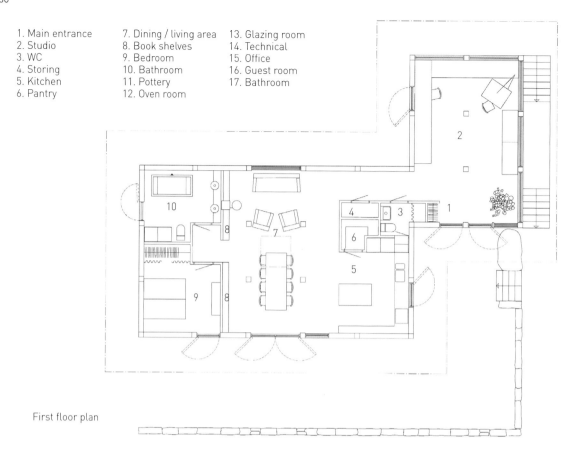

First floor plan

Basement plan

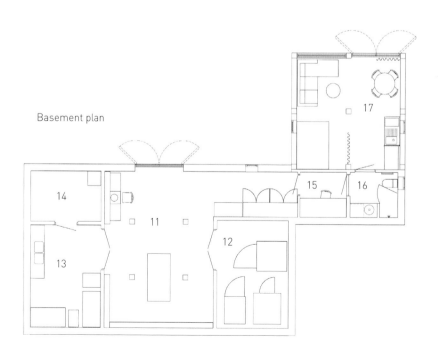

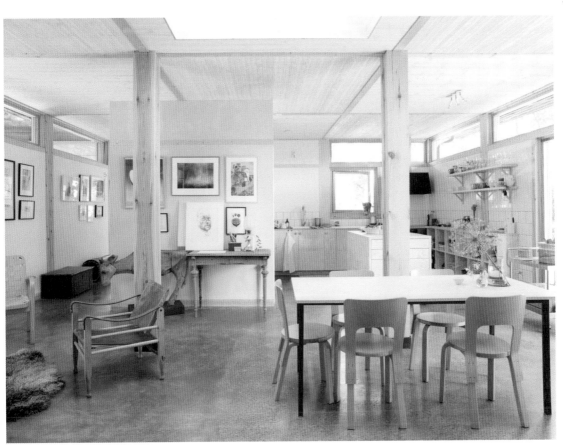

CASA PATIOS
EQUIPO DE ARQUITECTURA

www.equipodearquitectura.com.py
Project team: Horacio Cherniavsky, Viviana Pozzoli and José Cubilla
Location: Asunción, Paraguay
Total built area: 450 m2
Photo credits: © Leonardo Mendez, Federico Cairoli, Lauro Rocha
Structural engeneering: Enrique Granada + Emilio Richer

Starting from a structural scheme defined by beams with large spans, the dwelling develops on one level and extends over a sequence of spaces and courtyards that allows cross ventilation of all the rooms and is articulated by means of a circulation axis that becomes the backbone of the building. The roofs also function as patios, thus understanding the terrain as a succession of spaces at different heights. The creation of large openings creates a spatial continuity that links the natural with the artificial environment. The ceramic vaults provide the interior with a spatial quality appropriate for the region's climate. The use of the bioclimatic strategies adopted, green roofs, crossed ventilation, rainwater collection and solar protection, responds to the needs derived from the climatic conditions of Asunción.

Partiendo de un esquema estructural definido por vigas de grandes luces, la vivienda se desarrolla en un nivel y se extiende en una secuencia de espacios y patios que permite la ventilación cruzada de todos los ambientes y que se articula mediante un eje de circulación que se convierte en la espina dorsal del edificio. Las cubiertas funcionan también como patios, entendiendo así al terreno como una sucesión de patios a distintas alturas. La creación de grandes luces crea una continuidad espacial que entrelaza el entorno natural con el artificial. Las bóvedas cerámicas dotan al interior de una calidad espacial apropiada para el clima de la región. El uso de las estrategias bioclimáticas adoptadas: cubiertas verdes, ventilación cruzada, recolección de aguas pluviales y protección solar, responde a las necesidades derivadas de las condiciones climáticas de Asunción.

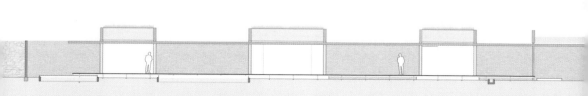

A-A section

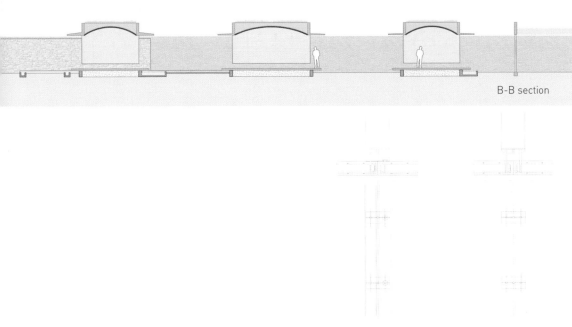

B-B section

Tensioner joint detail

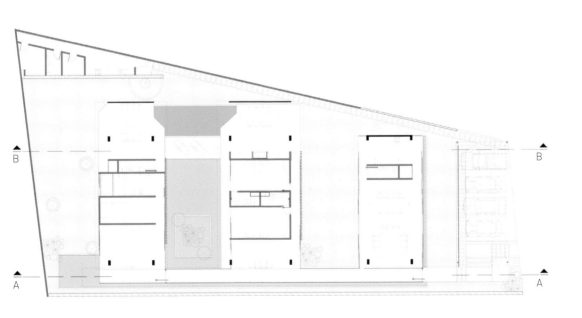

Floor plan

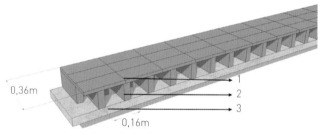

0,36m

0,16m

1. Tejuelita
2. Semi-pressed brick
3. Prestressed concrete base

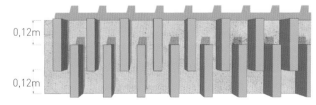

0,12m

0,12m

Lattice construction details

CRAYON HOUSE
GRIEVE GILLETT ANDERSEN

www.ggand.com.au
Project team: Dimitty Andersen, Tim Fenton, Sam Jeyaseelan, Garth Davos
Location: Goodwood, South Australia, Australia
Total built area: 200 m2
Photo credits: © Sam Noonan

Driven by the client's passion for sustainability, this house has an energy-con- scious soul. While it is sustainably responsible, it has a 'life is meant to be fun' attitude, expressed by a playfulness between light and colour depending on the change of seasons. Integral to the sustainable design is its 200 m2 footprint that can adapt as the young urban family grows and changes.
The house features two contrasting, yet complimentary house forms. A warm grey metal shape sits close to a timber form, and the glass entry blurs the lines between inside and outside. The metal house contains cooking, eating and socialising spaces.
The timber house is organised by a lofty corridor with high-level openable windows and contains two bedrooms and a utilities block that slides into a study. The garden design circles the house creating beautiful backdrops and functional outdoor living

Impulsada por la pasión del cliente por la sostenibilidad, esta casa tiene un alma consciente de la energía. Si bien es sosteniblemente responsable, tiene una actitud de «la vida es para divertirse», expresada por una actitud de juego entre la luz y el color, dependiendo del cambio de estaciones. Una parte integral del diseño sostenible es este espacio de 200 m2 que puede adaptarse a medida que la joven familia urbana crece y cambia.
La casa cuenta con dos formas de casa que contrastan, pero que son complementarias. Una cálida forma de metal gris se asienta cerca de una forma de madera, y la entrada de vidrio difumina las líneas entre el interior y el exterior. La casa de metal contiene espacios para cocinar, comer y socializar.
La casa de madera está organizada por un elevado pasillo con ventanas de alto nivel que se abren y contiene dos dormitorios y un bloque de utilidades que se desliza en un estudio. El diseño del jardín rodea la casa creando hermosos telones de fondo y una vida funcional al aire libre

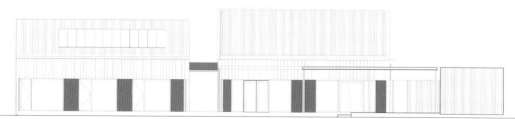

Elevation

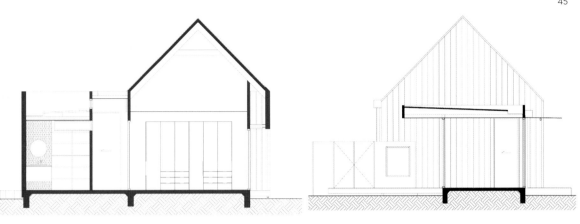

Section A   Section B

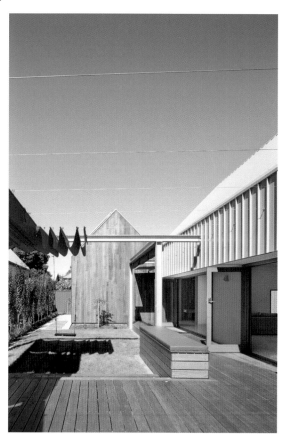

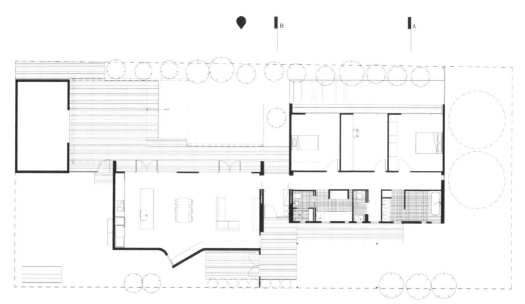

Floor plan

STRECKHOF WITH DESTILLERY
JURI TROY ARCHITECTS

www.juritroy.com
Project team: Juri Troy, Angelo Ferrara, Timea Kos
Location: Weingraben, Austria
Total built area: 95 m2
Floor area: 137 m2
Photo credits: © Juri Troy

The existing "Streckhof" of the family should be extended by a residential house. The building sits carefully between the neighboring barns and uses the same materials: wood and brick.

The gable walls consist of 50 cm burnt vertically perforated brick, which is plastered on the outside with uncoloured lime cement and on the inside with clay lime. The entire upper floor and attic, as well as the folding shutters are made of domestic silver fir. Handmade tiles and insulating materials made from renewable raw materials complete the material concept, which is based on natural building materials. Due to the generously openable, foldable slid- ing glazing on both sides, the entire living area can be opened to the garden, providing great natural ventilation in the warm summer months.

In the existing Barn next to it, the owner's distillery was installed as a restrained, dark colored spruce box.

Esta «streckhof» (construcción típica austriaca) de familia debía ser ampliada con una vivienda. El edificio se asienta cuidadosamente entre los graneros vecinos y utiliza los mismos materiales: madera y ladrillo.

Las paredes frontales están hechas de ladrillo quemado perforado verticalmente de 50 cm, enlucido con cemento calcáreo incoloro por fuera y cal arcillosa en el interior. Toda la planta superior y el ático, así como las persianas plegables, están hechas de madera de abeto. Las baldosas hechas a mano y los materiales aislantes de materias primas renovables completan el concepto, que se basa en materiales de construcción naturales. Gracias al acristalamiento corredizo plegable y de apertura generosa a ambos lados, toda la superficie habitable puede abrirse al jardín, lo que proporciona una gran ventilación natural en los cálidos meses de verano. En el granero existente, junto a esta, se instaló la destilería del propietario a modo de caja de pino y abeto de color oscuro.

Site plan

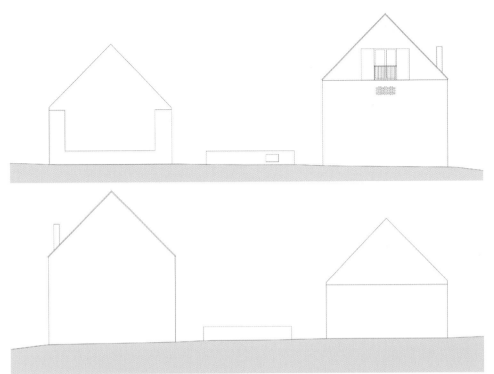

Elevations

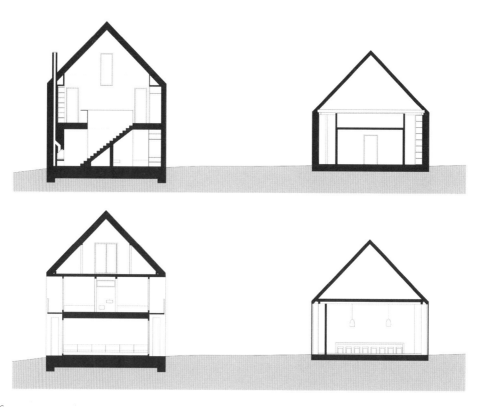

Sections

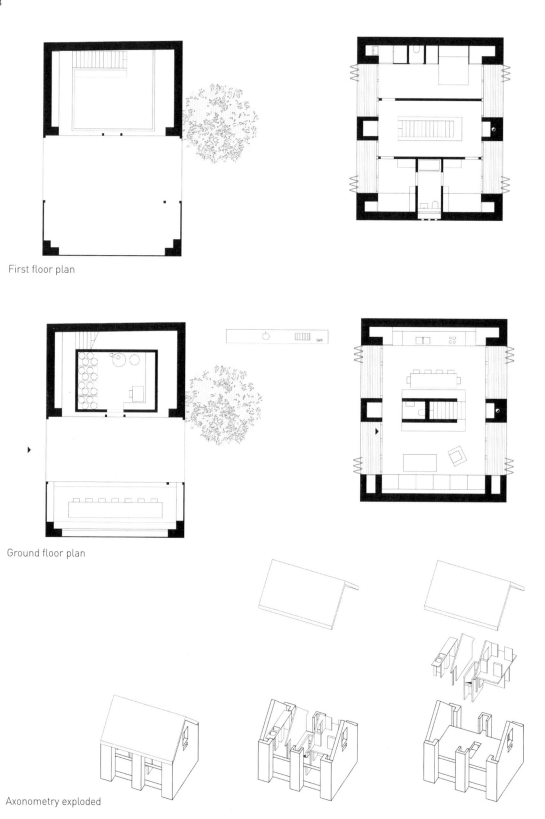

First floor plan

Ground floor plan

Axonometry exploded

HILLSIDE DOUPLEX
MWARCHITEKTEN

www.MWArch.org
Project team: Lukas Mähr, Carmen Wurz
Location: Schützenstrasse 3, 6845, Hohenems, Austria
Total built area: 250 m2
Photo credits: © Adolf Bereuter

Based on the budget and the desire to create sustainable housing, the decision was made to build a semi-detached house of two entities. The goal was to create an ecological architecture that does not fall into sterility and artificiality. As a model for this purpose the architects studied housing typologies that have been developed over generations. The facade design is based on the atmospheric qualities of these traditional structures. In the interior space, the hillside becomes noticeable in steps towards the living room and the terrace. Despite its simple timber frame structure insulated with cellulose the compact volume causes the house an excellent energy balance. The lowenergy house is heated by a geothermal heat pump. Instead of an artificial ventilation there is a fully programmable skylight at the highest point of the staircase providing fresh air and night cooling.

Basándose en el presupuesto y en el deseo de crear una vivienda sostenible, se decidió construir una casa adosada de dos usos. El objetivo era crear una arquitectura ecológica que no cayera en la esterilidad y la artificialidad. Como modelo para este propósito, los arquitectos estudiaron las tipologías de viviendas que se han desarrollado a lo largo de generaciones. El diseño de la fachada se basa en las cualidades atmosféricas de estas estructuras tradicionales. En el espacio interior, la ladera se hace visible en pasos hacia el salón y la terraza. A pesar de su sencilla estructura de madera aislada con celulosa, el volumen compacto hace que la casa tenga un excelente balance energético. La casa de bajo consumo de energía es calentada por una bomba de calor geotérmica. En lugar de ventilación artificial, se instaló una claraboya totalmente programable en el punto más alto de la escalera que proporciona aire fresco y refrigeración nocturna.

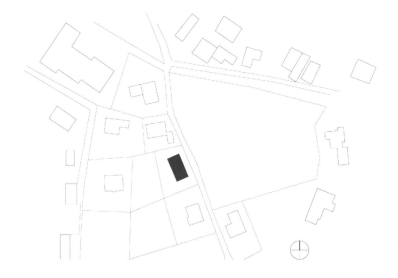

Site plan

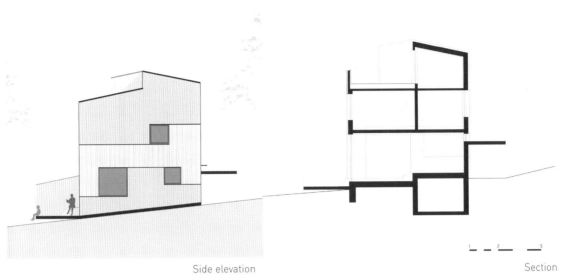

Side elevation   Section

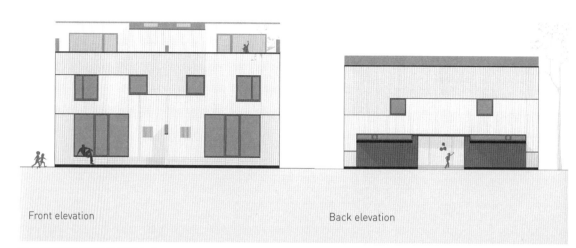

Front elevation   Back elevation

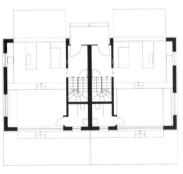

Ground floor plan

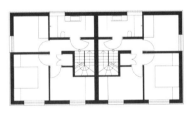

First floor plan

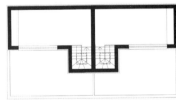

Second floor plan

CASA HOLMES FUENTEALBA
PFENNIGER & ASOCIADOS

www. pfennigerarquitectura.cl
Project team: Francis Pfenniger & Valeria Verlezza
Location: Yutuy – Chiloé - Chile
Total built area: 155 m2
Photo credits: © Carlos Hevia Riera, Lorena González V.,
Benjamín Holmes

The project is conceived as a refuge from the local climate and as a viewpoint over the Castro Channel. The building constitutes a simple volume with a common geometry in the area, which is located on a hillside and sits on piles, thus reducing its footprint on the ground.

The orientation of the house towards the views to the south made it necessary to foresee controlled openings in the rest of the façades to take advantage of sunlight. The construction reused waste materials from fish and mussels farming, abundant on the coast, and materials from domestic recycling.

Using a local strategy, a continuous watertight outer skin was proposed to fa cilitate the evacuation of rainwater. Indoor conditioning is achieved with a traditional Chiloé wood-burning stove and a low-consumption one, reinforced by the important insulation of the construction.

El proyecto se concibe como refugio frente al clima local y como mirador sobre el canal de Castro. El edificio constituye un volumen simple con una geometría común en la zona, que se sitúa en una ladera y se asienta sobre pilotes, reduciendo así su huella sobre el terreno.

La orientación de la casa hacia las vistas al sur hizo necesario prever aberturas controladas en el resto de fachadas para aprovechar la luz solar. La construcción reutilizó materiales de desecho de la piscicultura y mitilicultura, abundantes en la costa, y materiales procedentes del reciclaje doméstico.

Usando una estrategia local, se propuso una piel exterior estanca continua que facilitase la evacuación del agua de lluvia. La climatización interior se consigue con una tradicional cocina a leña de Chiloé y una estufa de leña de bajo consumo, reforzadas por el importante aislamiento de la envolvente.

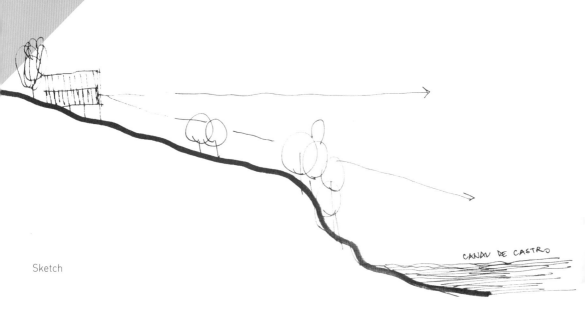

CANAL DE CASTRO

Sketch

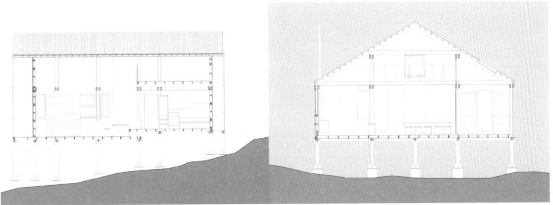

Longitudinal section

Cross section

64

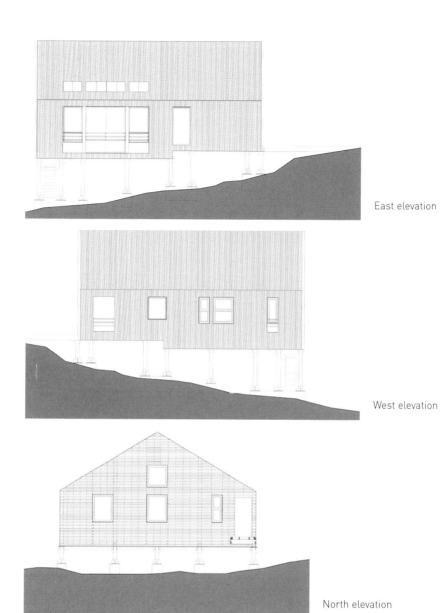

East elevation

West elevation

North elevation

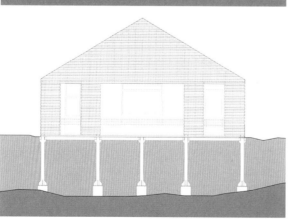

South elevation

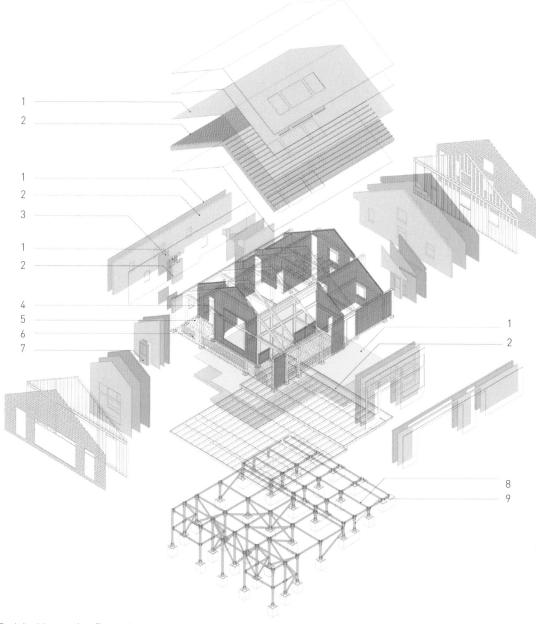

Exploited Isometrics. Re used materials

1. Tetrapack packaging
2. Expanded polystyrene
3. Wood recovered from spring
4. Wooden pallets
5. Salmon cage aisle
6. Salmon cage railing
7. Demolition doors
8. 150/50/4 mm galvanized beams with Weimaster type salmon cage structure.
9. Galvanized pillars d: 150 x 5mm structure salmon cage type Proma

Floor plan

Detail: wall with Zincalum floor/coating

1. Tetrapack moisture barrier overlapped.
2. Steep 5 × 7 cm @ 400 mm.
3. Zincalum steel plate e=0.4 mm.
4. Horizontal strip 2,5 × 7 cm @ 50 mm.
5. Pallet boarding 2,5 × 7 cm (vertical)
6. Vertical strip 2,5 × 5 cm @ 50 mm.
7. Tetrapack moisture barrier stapled to boarding with overlap. Aluminised face to exterior.
8. Expanded polystyrene e=100 mm.
9. External cladding plate Zincalum.
10. Polyethylene vapour barrier 0.2 mm.
11. Pallet boarding 2,5 × 7 cm (vertical)
12. Pallet frame.
13. External cladding plate Zincalum e 0.4 m.
14. Tetrapack moisture barrier stapled to boarding with overlap. Aluminised face to exterior.
15. Horizontal strip 2,5 × 7 cm @ 50 mm.
16. Expanded polystyrene e=100 mm or total width.
17. Vertical strip 2,5 × 5 cm @ 50 mm.
18. Galvanized steel master beams 150 × 50 × 5 mm.
19. Cutter profile zincalum e=0.4 mm.
20. 20 × 20 cm post.
21. Tarred sheathing.
22. Foundation support 0,60 × 0,60 × 0,8 m.
23. Planted poor concrete.
24. 5 x 5 cm @60 cm under steep.
25. 7 x 10 cm beam.
26. Ceiling plywood 10 mm.
27. Master Beam 2 (7 × 20 cm)
28. Master Beam 2 (5 × 25 cm)
29. Polyethylene vapour barrier 0.2 mm.
30. Plywood cladding 10 mm.
31. Pallet frame.
32. Boarding 3,7 × 10 cm tongue and groove.
33. Expanded polystyrene e=100 mm (min)
34. Polyethylene vapour barrier 0.3 mm.
35. Beam 2 (2" × 6") @ 0,6 m (tip)
36. Felt paper moisture barrier.

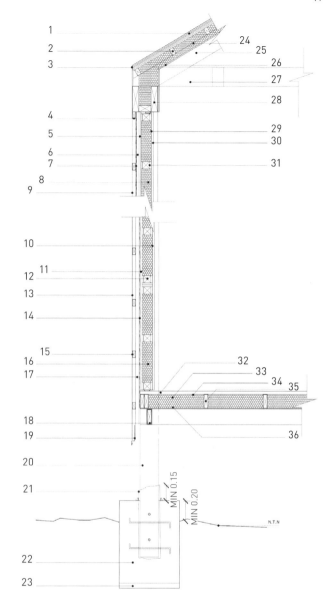

EL CAMAROTE
SEBASTIÁN CALERO LARREA

www.sebastiancalerolarrea.com
Architects: Sebastián Calero Larrea
Project team: Miguel Calero Castro (architectural design)
Location: Conocoto, DMQ
Total built area: 165 m2
Photo credits: © JAG Studio. © Sebastián Calero Larrea

This low-cost housing project on the outskirts of Quito attempts to reconstruct the idea of a local architecture that has been erased and replaced by an intrusive and serial housing typology. It consists of two elevated concrete platforms, a wooden skeleton and a mixed skin of brick, metal, glass and wood that encloses a topography of spaces that differentiates public from private areas. The relationship of the interior with the vegetation, and the fusion between structure, skin and space, always under the guidance of the manufacture of small details, are the main achievements of the project. As a consequence a great atlas of pieces and singular mechanisms emerges becoming an essential part of this project. These artisan conditions give the house an atmosphere of warmth and cosiness, very typical of a country home.

El proyecto de esta vivienda de bajo coste en las afueras de Quito intenta reconstruir la idea de una arquitectura lugareña que se ha ido borrando y ha sido reemplazada por una tipología habitacional intrusa y en serie. Se compone de dos plataformas elevadas de hormigón, un esqueleto de madera y una piel mixta de ladrillo, metal, vidrio y madera que encierra una topografía de espacios que diferencia las áreas públicas de las privadas. La relación del interior con la vegetación, y la fusión entre estructura, piel y espacio, siempre bajo la guía de la manufactura de pequeños detalles, son los principales logros del proyecto. Como consecuencia surge un gran atlas de piezas y mecanismos singulares que son parte esencial de este proyecto. Estas condiciones artesanales imprimen a la vivienda una atmósfera de calidez y domesticidad, muy propias de una casa de campo.

Sketch

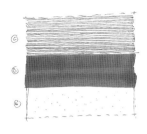

Sketch

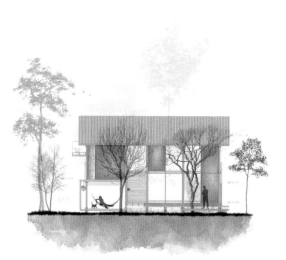

Front view

Rear view

Right side vew

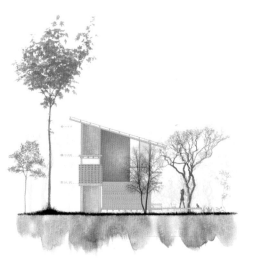

Left side view

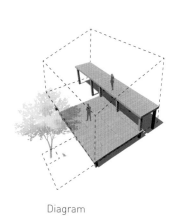
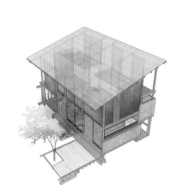
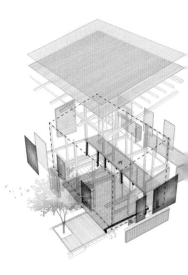

Diagram

SOFA (SOUTH FACE)
KT814 ARCHITECTURE

www.kt814.com
Project team: Rich Assenberg, Nathan Gray – kt814
Location: Teton County, WY
Total built area: Main floor 173 m2, Second floor 184 m2,
Garage 76 m2
Photo credits: © David Agnello, kt814

Conceived as a reflection of the beautiful natural environment in which it is located, this house receives its name from the orientation (So-uth Fa-ced) of all its rooms, which allows abundant direct sunlight, a factor that is one of the engines of the project. For this purpose, it is structured in three twin volumes that create a great variety of interior and exterior spaces, through which light is filtered, and whose Douglas fir cladding evokes the granaries of the area. The project uses design principles of a passive house. By means of measures such as highly insulated enclosures, the green roof over the lower volume, high-performance windows or solar panels that in summer generate 90% of the demand for hot water, it responds to the intention of customers to build a home with the highest possible energy efficiency.

Concebida como un reflejo del hermoso entorno natural en el que se ubica, esta casa recibe su nombre de la orientación (So-uth Fa-ced) de todas sus estancias, que permite la entrada abundante de luz solar directa, factor que constituye uno de los motores del proyecto. Para ello se estructura en tres volúmenes maclados que crean una gran variedad de espacios interiores y exteriores, a través de los cuales se filtra la luz, y cuyo revestimiento de abeto Douglas evoca los graneros de la zona. El proyecto utiliza principios de diseño de una casa pasiva. Mediante medidas como cerramientos altamente aislados, la cubierta verde sobre el volumen inferior, ventanas de alto rendimiento o paneles solares que en verano generan el 90% de la demanda de agua caliente, se da respuesta a la intención de los clientes de construir una vivienda con la mayor eficiencia energética posible.

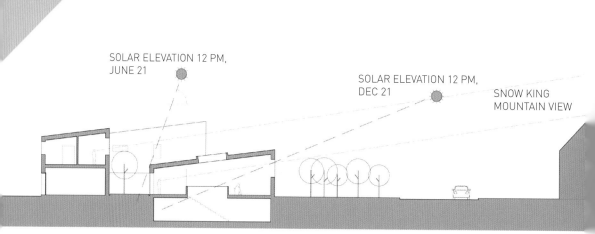

SOLAR ELEVATION 12 PM, JUNE 21

SOLAR ELEVATION 12 PM, DEC 21

SNOW KING MOUNTAIN VIEW

Section

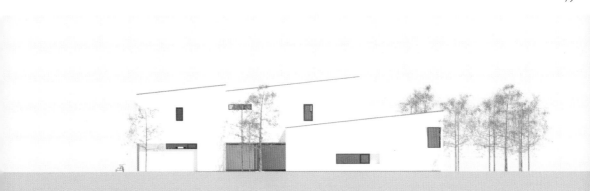

West elevation

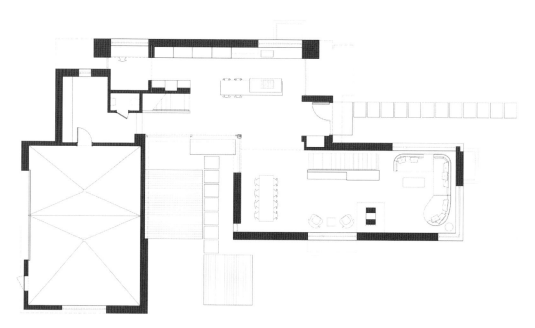

Ground floor plan

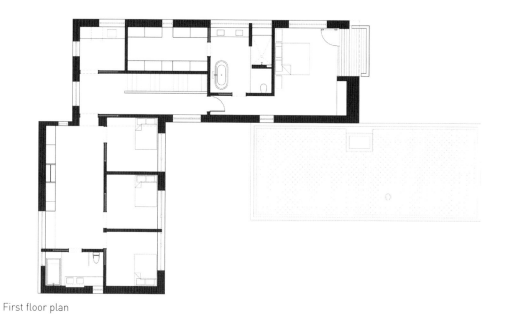

First floor plan

0   5   15   N

HOUSE OF FIR
KT814 ARCHITECTURE

www.kt814.com
Project team: Nathan Gray, Rich Assenberg – kt814
Location: Teton County, WY
Total built area: 297 m2 (232 m2 habitable – 65 m2 garage)
Photo credits: © David Agnello

Under the imposing gaze of the Grand Teton Mountains and with an image inspired by the agricultural buildings of the area, the project of this passive house expresses its respect for the natural environment in which it is located. The position of the building and its design are aimed at minimising the impact on existing nature, preserving privacy with respect to neighbouring houses and offering ample views from the inside.
The house is organised into three pavilions lined with cedar and Douglas pine differentiated by use: suite, main-garage, guest room and a living room- kitchen-dining room, connected to each other by means of transition spaces that capture moments in the landscape. The passive design strategies used, coupled with low maintenance costs and the application of Universal Design principles make this house a model of sustainability.

Bajo la imponente mirada de las montañas Grand Teton y con una imagen inspirada en los edificios agrícolas de la zona, el proyecto de esta casa pasiva manifiesta su respeto por el entorno natural en el que se sitúa. La posición del edificio y su diseño tienen como objetivo minimizar el impacto sobre la naturaleza existente, preservar la privacidad respecto de las casas vecinas y ofrecer amplias vistas desde el interior.
La casa se organiza en tres pabellones revestidos de cedro y pino Douglas diferenciados por el uso: suite principal-garaje, suite de invitados y una sala de estar-cocina-comedor, conectados entre sí mediante espacios de transición que capturan momentos en el paisaje. Las estrategias de diseño pasivo utilizadas, unidas a los bajos costes de mantenimiento y a la aplicación de los principios de Diseño Universal hacen de esta casa un modelo de sostenibilidad.

South elevation

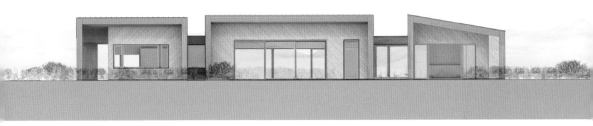

North elevation

SOLAR ELEVATION 12 PM,
JUNE 21

SOLAR ELEVATION 12 PM,
DEC 21

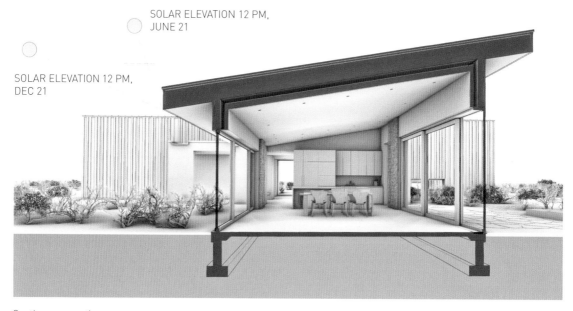

Section perspective

West elevation

East elevation

BELLBIRD RETREAT
STEENDIJK

www.steendijk.com
Project team: Brian Steendijk, Shaun Crossman, Timo Lueck
Location: Killarney, Queensland, Australia
Total built area: 67 m2
Photo credits: © Christopher Frederick Jones, Brian Steendyk,
Craig Hodges

This weekend home in a forest reserve fosters a dialogue between the natural and man-made environment through form and materials, climate sensitivity and the structure of views. Three pivoting brick walls define the organic shape of the house, shortening the perception of the façade and protecting it from southern winds, rain and fire. Inside, the space expands through a continuous boomerang shaped glass façade to blend in with the landscape. The thermal mass of the three-layer walls and the concrete slab minimizes temperature fluctuations in the interior. The pleated steel corten roof channels supply water to the house, offering a simple structural solution that allows for a northfacing overhang and has a maintenance-free finish.

Esta vivienda de fin de semana situada en una reserva forestal fomenta un diálogo entre el entorno natural y el creado por el hombre a través de la forma y los materiales, la sensibilidad climática y la estructura de las vistas. Tres muros de ladrillo pivotantes definen la forma orgánica de la casa, acortando la percepción de la fachada, y la protegen de los vientos del sur, la lluvia y los incendios. En el interior, el espacio se expande a través de una fachada continua de vidrio en forma de bumerán para mezclarse con el paisaje. La masa térmica de los muros de tres capas y de la losa de hormigón minimiza las fluctuaciones de temperatura en el interior. La cubierta plisada de acero corten canaliza el agua hacia los tanques que abastecen la casa, ofrece una solución estructural simple que permite un voladizo orientado a norte y presenta un acabado sin mantenimiento.

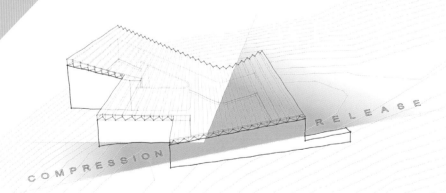

Concept diagram

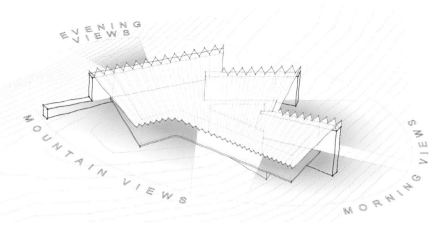

EVENING VIEWS

MOUNTAIN VIEWS

MORNING VIEWS

View diagram

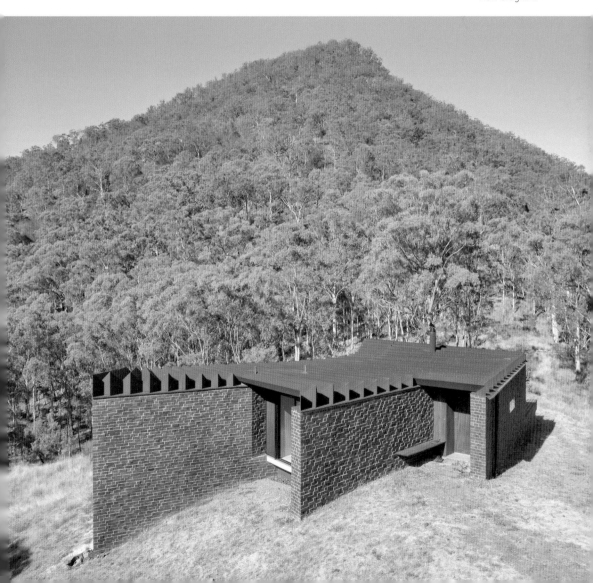

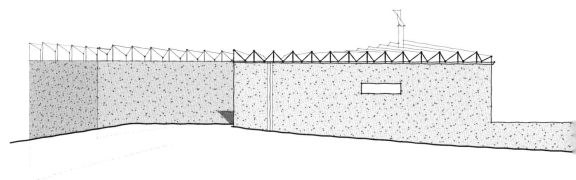

South elevation

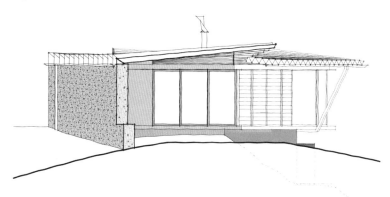

East elevation

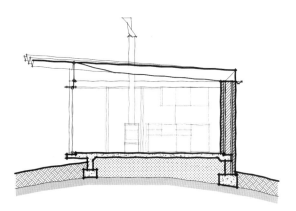

Cross section

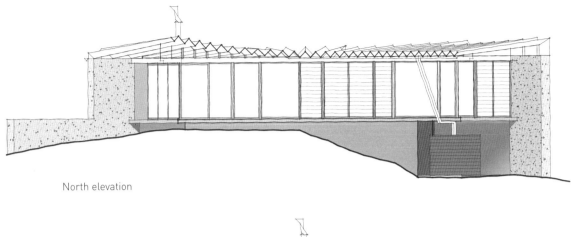

North elevation

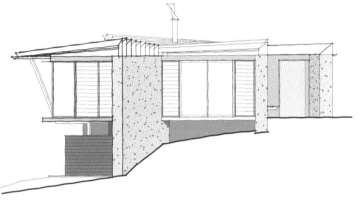

West elevation

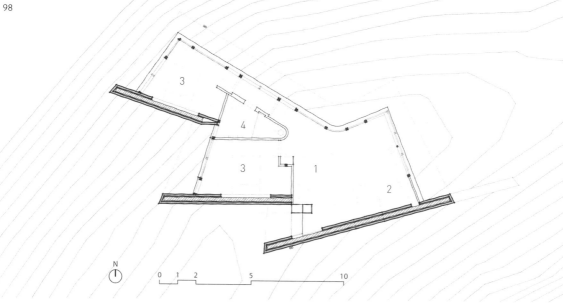

Floor plan

1. Living
2. Kitchen
3. Bedroom
4. Bathroom

BOSVILLA
NATRUFIED ARCHITECTURE

www.natrufied.com
Project team: Boris Zeisser with Anja Verdonk and Klaas J de Jong
Location: Bergen (NH), the Netherlands
Total built area: 400 m2
Photo credits: © Christian Richters, Berlin/Boris Zeisser, Bergen

The project includes the construction of a house, a garden house, a car park and another for bicycles, designed to preserve and capture the natural environment. The house has a completely open upper floor with the common áreas. This area textends the natural environment towards the interior. The ground floor, which contains the bedrooms, is embedded in the land providing greater privacy. The different types of wood that make up the main structure, together with the rest of the materials used, generate a soft palette of natural tones. In addition to using materials that absorb CO2 such as wood and bamboo, the house has great thermal insulation in its enclosures and openings, along with a green roof that also collects rainwater and houses 35 solar panels.

El proyecto comprende la construcción de una vivienda, una casa de jardín, un aparcamiento de coches y otro para bicicletas, diseñados para preservar y capturar el entorno natural. La vivienda presenta una planta superior completamente abierta, destinada a las zonas comunes, presidida por una cubierta en vuelo que prolonga el entorno natural hacia el interior. La planta inferior, que contiene los dormitorios, se incrusta en el terreno brindando una mayor privacidad. Los diferentes tipos de maderas que conforman la estructura principal, junto al resto de materiales utilizados, generan una paleta suave de tonos naturales. Además de utilizar materiales que absorben CO2 como la madera y el bambú, la casa presenta un gran aislamiento térmico en sus cerramientos y aberturas, conjuntamente con una cubierta verde que también recoge el agua de lluvia y alberga 35 paneles solares.

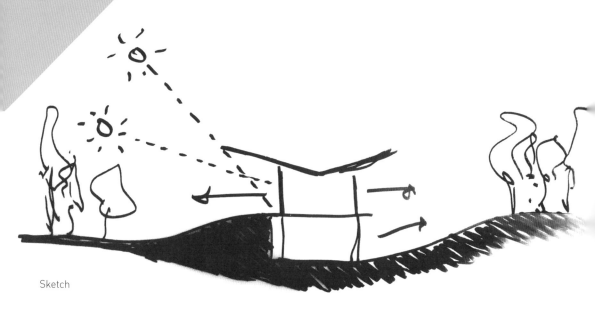

Sketch

Site plan

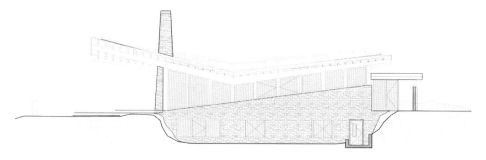

North elevation

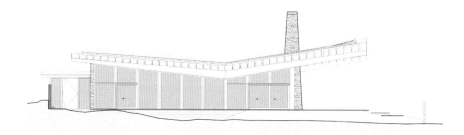

South elevation

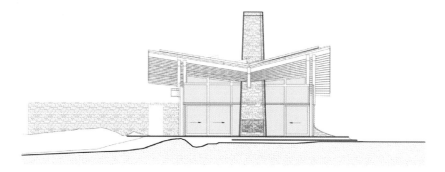

East elevation

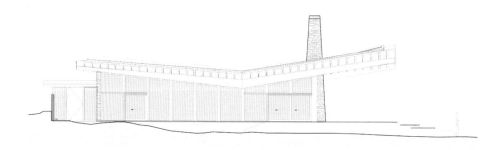

West elevation

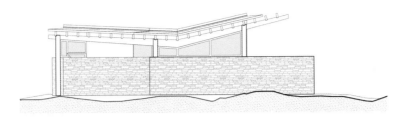

Garden house. North elevation

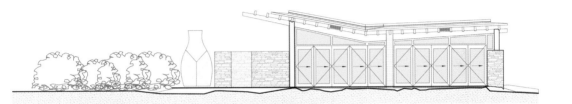

Garden house. South elevation

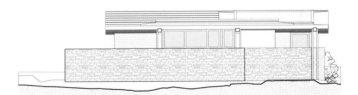

Garden house. East elevation

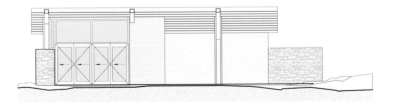

Garden house. West elevation

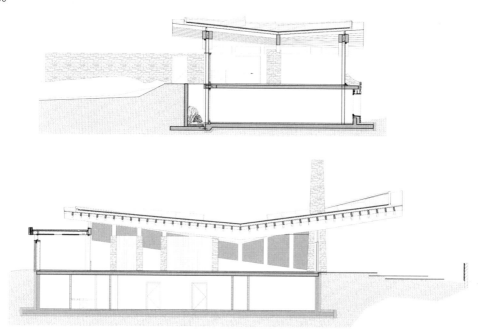

Sections

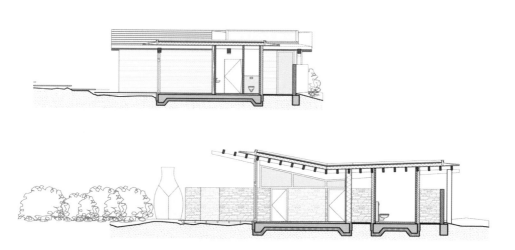

Garden house. Sections

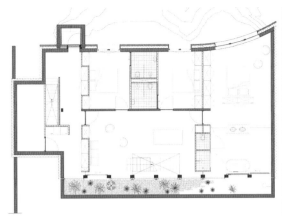

First floor plan

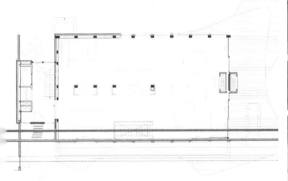

Ground floor plan

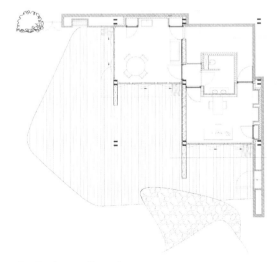

Garden house. Floor plan

RENOVATION OF MILL AND CONVERSION INTO HOUSING
STEMPEL TESAŘ ARCHITEKTI

www.stempel-tesar.com
Project team: Ján Stempel, Jan Jakub Tesaˇr, Aleš Herold
Location: Slapy, Czech Republic
Total built area: 241 m2
Photo credits: © Filip Šlapal

The reconversion into a house of this old mill located next to a pond was a radical action that revitalized the building but retained its charm. The main action consisted of creating a courtyard that allowed light to enter through a transverse glazed enclosure and interior ventilation, necessary to reduce the constant humidity that threatened the house. For this purpose, a strip of the central part was avoided thus preserving the original imprint of the building. The existing wooden structure of the roof was dismantled, renovated and repositioned in its place, leaving a view along the continuous space developed between the two upper floors. The reconversion involved a careful and gradual renovation or replacement of the various elements of the mill to meet the objective of preserving the beauty of the old construction.

La reconversión en vivienda de este antiguo molino situado junto a un estanque supuso una actuación radical que revitalizó el edificio pero conservó su encanto. La principal actuación consistió en crear un patio que permitiese la entrada de luz a través de un cerramiento transversal acristalado y la ventilación interior, necesaria para reducir la humedad constante que amenazaba la casa. Para ello se «amputó» una franja de la parte central, preservándose así la huella original del edificio. La estructura de madera existente del techo fue desmontada, renovada y recolocada en su lugar, dejándose vista a lo largo del espacio continuo desarrollado entre las dos plantas superiores. La reconversión comportó una renovación cuidadosa y gradual o el reemplazo de los diversos elementos del molino para cumplir con el objetivo de preservar la belleza del antiguo edificio.

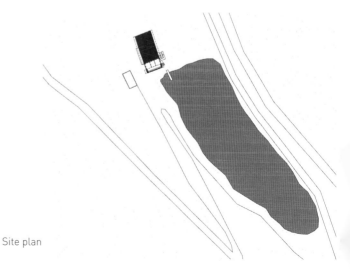

Site plan

Sketches

Sketches

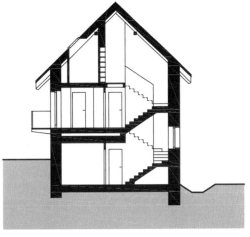

Section

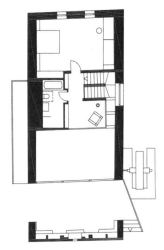

First floor plan

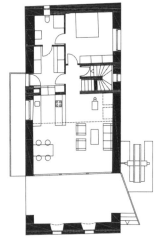

Ground floor plan

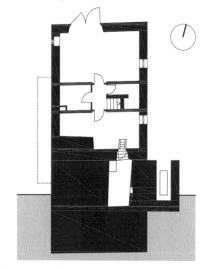

Basement plan

VALLEY HOUSE
SPARKS ARCHITECTS

www.sparksarchitects.com
Project team: Dan Sparks, Tommy Vuletic
Location: Montville, Queensland, Australia
Total built area: 256 m2
Photo credits: © Christopher Fredrick Jones

The dramatic topography, bush setting of the Obi Obi Valley and Kondalilla Falls; and diverse climatic conditions of the hinterland were the driving forces for this design. A simple pavilion form was adopted which allowed for a rational approach to planning and structure.
Precast concrete rainwater tanks act as thermal buffers and spatial dividers. The tanks are partially buried in the site to allow for small plywood 'bed nests' to sit above them, regaining the lost space of the tanks footprint. The tanks and their hoop pine nests become 'precious objects', protected by the robust outer shell of masonry, steel and glass. The draped roof of the building, a subtle echo of the site topography, allows for appropriate pitch and northern orientation for the photovoltaic array, direct rainwater feed to the internal tanks and appopriate shading for winter and summer sun angles.

La espectacular topografía, el entorno de arbustos del valle de Obi Obi y las cataratas de Kondalilla, y las diversas condiciones climáticas del interior fueron las fuerzas impulsoras de este diseño. Se adoptó una forma de pabellón sencilla que permitía un enfoque racional de la planificación y la estructura. Los depósitos de agua de lluvia prefabricados de hormigón actúan como amortiguadores térmicos y divisores espaciales. Los tanques están parcialmente enterrados en el sitio para permitir que los pequeños «nidos de cama» de madera contrachapada se asienten sobre ellos, recuperando el espacio perdido de la huella del tanque. Los tanques y sus nidos de pino se convierten en «objetos preciosos», protegidos por el robusto armazón exterior de mampostería, acero y vidrio. El tejado del edificio, un sutil eco de la topografía del lugar, permite una adecuada inclinación y orientación norte para el conjunto fotovoltaico, alimentación directa de agua de lluvia a los tanques internos y sombra adecuada para los ángulos de sol de invierno y verano.

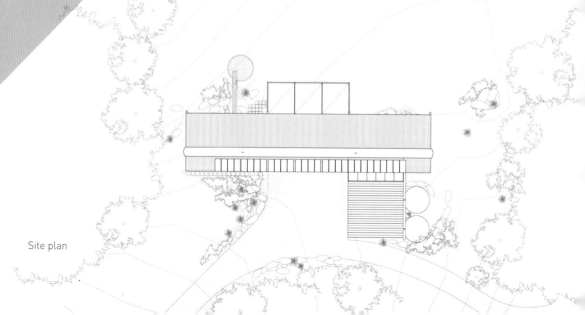

Site plan

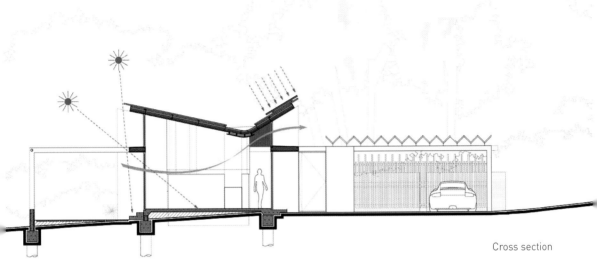

Cross section

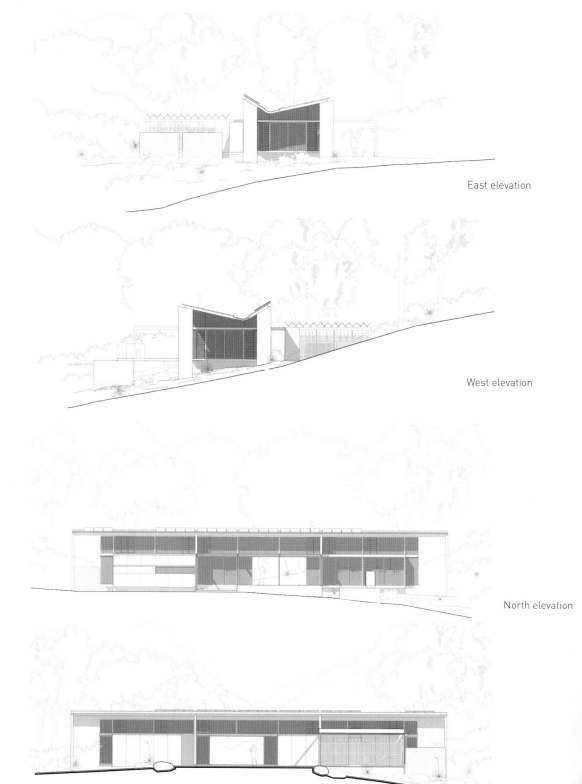

East elevation

West elevation

North elevation

South elevation

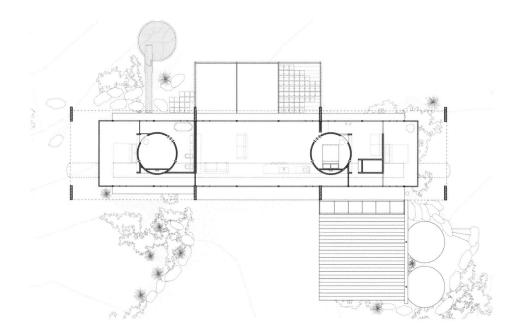

Mezzanine plan

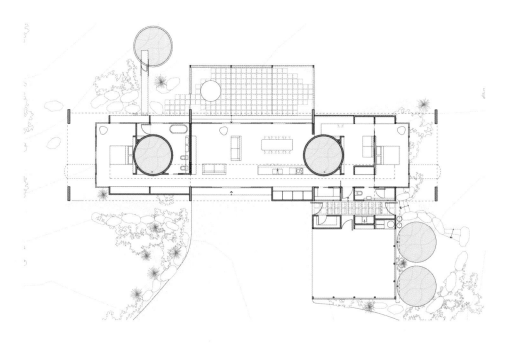

Ground floor plan

TENT HOUSE
SPARKS ARCHITECTS

www.sparksarchitects.com
Project team: Tent - Dan Sparks, Michael Cornish, Alex Keen
Location: Noosa Hinterland, Queensland, Australia
Total built area: 230 m2
Photo credits: © Christopher Fredrick Jones

The architecture of this dynamic building is based on a dual concept whereby a closed and insulated box in the coldest months is transformed, by opening its enclosures in the warmest months, into a new volumetry presided over by a translucent membrane with the form of a tent that contrasts with the dark colour of the box.

The design integrates sustainable strategies adapted to the site. The plant, simple and open, is located on an east-west axis that allows you to enjoy the views over the rainforest and maximize solar gain in winter. The natural cross ventilation is complemented by the additional ventilation generated between the tent and the pavilion. Rainwater collected in tanks is used for the general purpose of the house and to maintain the orchard. Trees felled during construction were reused in various carpentry elements.

La arquitectura de este dinámico edificio se basa en un concepto dual por el que una caja cerrada y aislada en los meses más fríos se transforma, al abrir sus cerramientos en los meses cálidos, en una nueva volumetría presidida por una membrana translúcida a modo de carpa que contrasta con el color oscuro de la caja.

El diseño integra estrategias sostenibles adecuadas al emplazamiento. La planta, simple y abierta, se sitúa sobre un eje este-oeste que permite disfrutar de las vistas sobre la selva tropical y maximizar la ganancia solar en invierno. La ventilación cruzada natural se complementa con la ventilación adicional generada entre la carpa y el pabellón. El agua de lluvia recolectada en tanques se utiliza para los fines generales de la casa y para mantener el huerto. Los árboles talados durante la construcción se reutilizaron en diversos elementos de carpintería.

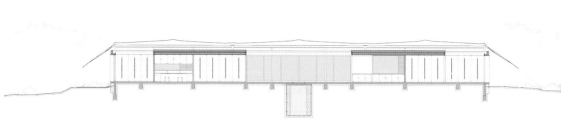

Section

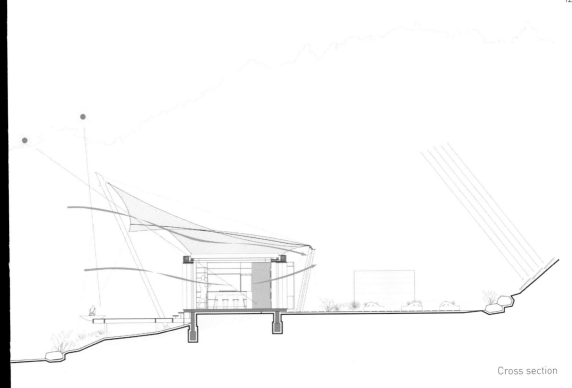

Cross section

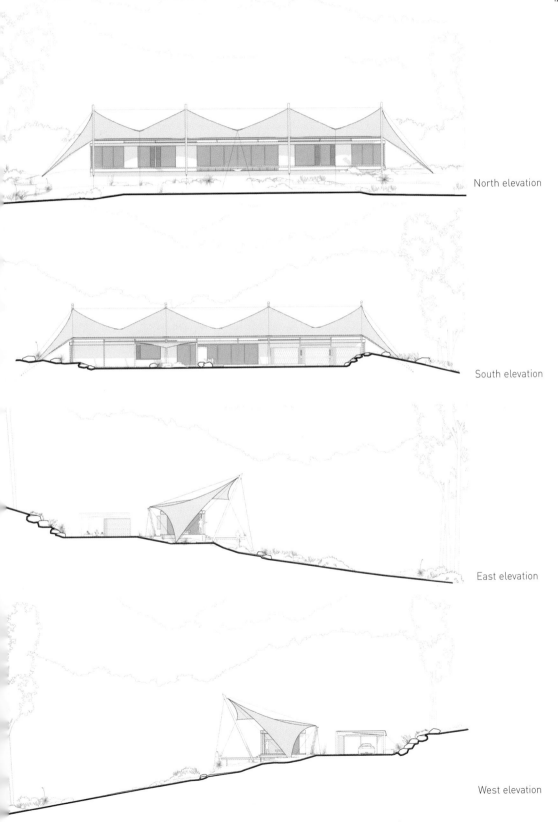

North elevation

South elevation

East elevation

West elevation

124

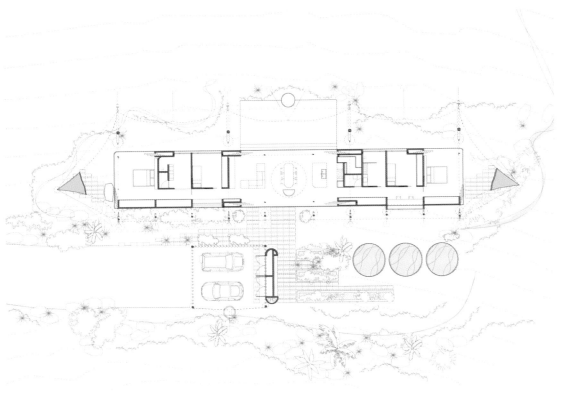

Floor plan

YERONGA HOUSE
TIM BENNETTON ARCHITECTS

www.timbennetton.com.au
Project team: Tim Bennetton, Ryan Bunn
Location: Yeronga, Queensland, Australia
Total built area: 150 m2
Photo credits: © Shantanu Starick

There were two main aims behind this renovation project. First, to solve problems commonly found in "Queenslander" timber houses: a dark and hot interior with poor ventilation and poor planning; and second to add a guest room and studio in the form of a new pavilion open towards the back garden. The project integrates the house into the landscape through new patios and stepped platforms that improve the relationship between interior and exterior. Sustainability was a priority for the clients. A new corridor through to the west side garden allows the interior to breathe, while a slatted awning regulates solar gain over that façade. Air conditioning was eliminated and natural ventilation and light entry was encouraged. Various water-sensitive urban design strategies are also incorporated, such as the permeable landscaped surfaces and the reuse of rainwater.

Este proyecto de renovación tenía dos objetivos principales. En primer lugar, para resolver los problemas que se encuentran comúnmente en las casas de madera «Queenslander»: un interior oscuro y caluroso con mala ventilación y mala planificación; y en segundo lugar, para añadir una habitación de huéspedes y un estudio en forma de un nuevo pabellón abierto hacia el jardín trasero. El proyecto integra la casa en el paisaje a través de nuevos patios y plataformas escalonadas que mejoran la relación entre interior y exterior. La sostenibilidad fue una prioridad para los clientes. Un nuevo corredor a través del jardín lateral oeste permite respirar al interior, mientras que un toldo de listones regula la ganancia solar sobre esa fachada. El aire acondicionado fue eliminado y se fomentó la ventilación natural y la entrada de luz. Se incorporan también diversas estrategias de diseño urbano sensible al agua, como las superficies ajardinadas permeables y la reutilización del agua de lluvia.

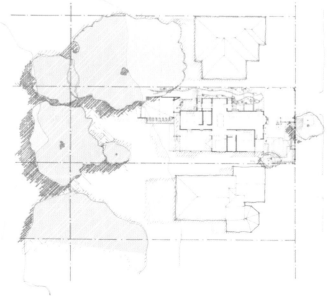

Site plan

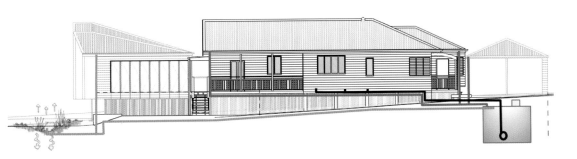

Water layout

Street elevation

Rear elevation

134

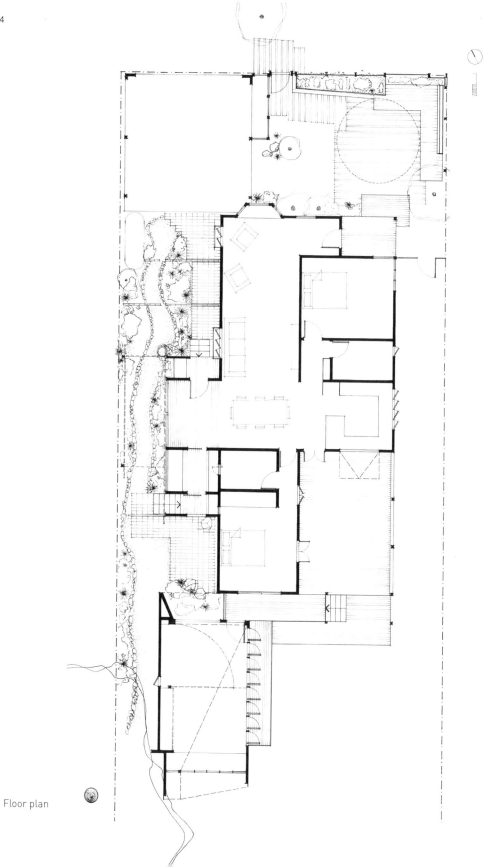

Floor plan

APPLE CRATE SHACK
AKA ARCHITECTS

www.aka-architects.com.au
Project team: Andrew Kerr, Geoff Clark
Location: Flowerpot, Tasmania, Australia
Total built area: 61 m2 enclosed, 20 m2 decks, 20 m2 patio
Photo credits: © Jordan Davis

The project follows a design that is guided by needs, not desires. A modest footprint but a generous volume satisfies all spatial and functional requirements. Circulation is efficient: strong connections extend the spaces to interact with the surrounding landscape.

The house is both experimentation and an investigation of ideas: the aesthetics of the "apple crate" refers to the local fruit industry. A limited palette of materials speaks of durability and economy.

The project develops passive solar design principles and encourages sustainable practices through elements such as photovoltaic panels, reverse-cycle heat pump, rainwater collection tanks, reuse of building materials and equipment, and the use of local materials.

El proyecto es una exploración de adecuación: el diseño se guía por necesidades, no por deseos. Una huella modesta pero un volumen generoso satisface todos los requisitos espaciales y funcionales. La circulación es sucinta y eficiente: las fuertes conexiones extienden los espacios para interactuar con el paisaje circundante.

La vivienda es también experimentación y una investigación de ideas: la estética de la «caja de manzanas» hace referencia a la industria frutícola local. Una paleta de materiales limitada habla de durabilidad y economía.

El proyecto desarrolla principios de diseño solar pasivo y fomenta las prácticas sostenibles mediante elementos tales como paneles fotovoltaicos, bomba de calor de ciclo inverso, tanques para recuperación de agua de lluvia, la reutilización de materiales de construcción y de equipos de instalaciones o el uso de materiales locales.

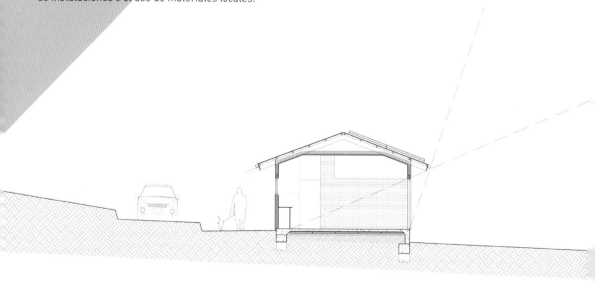

Section

0   1.2   5.7

East elevation

West elevation

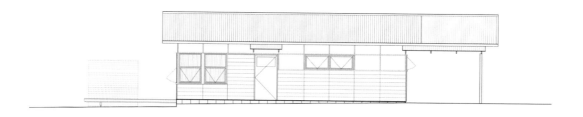

South elevation

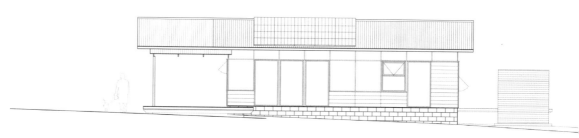

North elevation

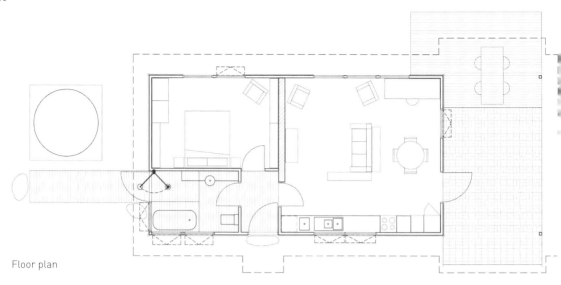

Floor plan